Study Guide for the US Citizenship Test in English

Mike Swedenberg

Study Guide
100 Questions and Answers for the US Immigration Test
in English
A unique product, professionally developed and annotated
Updated November 2015

The U.S. Citizenship Services (USCIS) administers a verbal test to all immigrants applying for citizenship. This study guide tutors those who are proficient in English and do not require a secondary language. The questions have been selected from questions used on past exams by the USCIS.

Studying these questions does not guarantee obtaining
citizenship to the United States.

Bi Lingual Languages available:
Spanish, Polish, French, Portuguese, Russian, Vietnamese and Tagalog.
In Print and eBooks at Amazon.com

ACKNOWLEDGMENTS

We gratefully acknowledge The U.S. Citizenship Services (USCIS) for their cooperation.

Good luck on the test.

CONTENTS

"I pledge allegiance to the flag of the United States of America, and to the republic for which it stands, one nation under God, indivisible, with liberty and justice for all."

INTRODUCTION

The 100 sample questions and answers for the US Immigration test are listed below. The test is an oral exam in which the USCIS Officer will ask the applicant up to 10 of the 100 questions. An applicant must answer six out of ten questions correctly to pass the civics portion of the test.

On the naturalization test, some answers may change because of elections or appointments. As you study for the test, make sure that you know the most current members of Congress, Senate, Speaker of the House and Governor of your state and district.

This publication is the only study guide that provides this information and updates it throughout the year.

We also provide you with the Sample Written Questions which all applicants must know how to write in English.

Advice from the Immigration Law offices of Christopher Kurczaba

6219 N Milwaukee Ave, Chicago, IL 60646

(773) 774-0011

KurczabaLaw@sbcglobal.net

Three Tests for Citizenship

Most applicants for citizenship or naturalization as it is called, are actually subject to THREE different "tests" when applying. It is important that an individual understand that in applying for Citizenship their entire immigration history is being reviewed and an Immigration Officer is making a determination not only over whether an applicant passes a test, but moreover, is reviewing the applicant's entire immigration history.

The Citizenship process should be looked upon as a complex, detailed demanding process, not just the completion of a form and passing of a simple civics test. This is not a process that should be taken lightly. Often persons get "free" help with benevolent charities completing applications during large scale meetings. However, an applicant can face severe consequences including the loss of their permanent residency and even removal from the United States if certain matters come to the attention of an Immigration Officer reviewing your application.

First and foremost are persons who have ever been arrested, detained or even stopped by a Police Officer. These individuals should ensure they seek the assistance of an attorney to review their criminal record before proceeding with the filing of an application for Citizenship.

Each Applicant for Citizenship undergoes three tests:

1. Test of Civics/History/Government, Reading & Writing

    a. Civics/history test of 10 questions chosen out of a possible 100

b. Reading – applicants will be asked to read out loud a sample sentence from a fixed set of possible sentences

c. Writing – applicants will be asked to write a sentence dictated by an Immigration Officer.

2. Ability to Communicate in English

a. The Immigration Officer will review your application with you. Traditionally, this takes place after you pass your test. This portion can be difficult for those that do not speak English well.

b. The Immigration Officer will speak to you in English to determine if you generally can communicate.

3. Eligibility –a review of an Applicant's personal history

a. The Immigration Officer will review your entire immigration file and determine if you have the proper character to become a citizen. The Officer will literally have before them your entire immigration history including every form and piece of paper that you submitted to the Immigration Service. This includes your applications for immigration benefits before permanent residency.

i. The Officer will review how you obtained your green card or permanent residency.

1. If you received your permanent residency through marriage to a US Citizen, then the Immigration Officer will ask questions about your marriage. The Officer can question whether the marriage was legitimate.

2. If you received your permanent residency through a family member – the Immigration Officer will review your original application to make sure there were no improprieties when you applied.

3. If you received your permanent residency through an employer – the Immigration Officer can ask you questions about the employer and the employment relationship.

ii. The Officer will review your criminal background – checking if you were ever arrested/detained/stopped by a Police Officer at home or abroad.

1. For the Immigration Service- to be stopped, arrested or detained means precisely that – any time a Police agency would take your fingerprints

a. Regardless of the eventual outcome of the case – or what you think it means to be arrested – you will be expected to admit to all times that you were arrested/stopped or detained by a Police agency.

i. Sometimes applicants believe that an arrest means serving time in jail. But the Immigration Service has a much broader interpretation – including anytime that a Police agency would take your fingerprints and record the information.

ii. The Immigration Service obtains criminal background information on individuals primarily from the FBI. The FBI retains this information forever, regardless of expungements, or local agencies clearing of a criminal history.

AMERICAN GOVERNMENT / GOBIERNO AMERICANO

I. Principles of American Democracy

1. What is the supreme law of the land?

> The Constitution

2. What does the Constitution do?

> Sets up the government
>
> Defines the government
>
> Protects basic rights of Americans

3. The idea of self-government is in the first three words of the Constitution. What are these words?

> We the People

4. What is an amendment?

> A change to the Constitution.
>
> An addition to the Constitution.

5. What do we call the first ten amendments to the Constitution?

> The Bill of Rights

6. What is one right or freedom from the First Amendment? (You need to know one answer)

Speech

Religion

Assembly

Press

Petition the government

7. How many amendments does the Constitution have?

Twenty-seven (27)

8. What did the Declaration of Independence do?

Announced our independence (from Great Britain)

Declared our independence (from Great Britain)

Said that the United States is free (from Great Britain)

9. What are two rights in the Declaration of Independence?

Life

Liberty

Pursuit of Happiness

10. What is freedom of religion?

You can practice any religion, or not practice a religion.

11. What is the economic system in the United States?*

capitalist economy

market economy

12. What is the "rule of law"?

Everyone must follow the law

Leaders must obey the law.

Government must obey the law.

No one is above the law

B. System of Government

13. Name one branch or part of the government.*

    Congress

    Legislative

    President

    Executive

    The courts

    Judicial

14. What stops one branch of government from becoming too powerful?

    Checks and balances

    Separation of powers

15. Who is in charge of the executive branch?

    The President

16. Who makes federal laws?

    Congress

    Senate and House (of Representatives)

    (U.S. or national) legislature

17. What are the two parts of the U.S. Congress?*

The Senate and House (of Representatives)

18. How many U.S. Senators are there?

One hundred (100)

19. We elect a U.S. Senator for how many years?

Six (6)

20. Who is one of your state's U.S. Senators?*

See Page 26

* If you are 65 years old or older and have been a legal permanent resident of the United States for 20 or more years, you may study just the questions that have been marked with an asterisk.

21. The House of Representatives has how many voting members?

Four hundred thirty-five (435)

22. We elect a U.S. Representative for how many years?

Two (2)

23. Name your U.S. Representative.

Answers will vary. [Residents of territories with nonvoting Delegates or resident Commissioners may provide the name of that Delegate or Commissioner. Also acceptable is any statement that the territory has no (voting) Representatives in Congress.]

See Page 29

24. Who does a U.S. Senator represent?

    All people of the state

25. Why do some states have more Representatives than other states?

    There are three correct answers. You need to know one answer.

    Because of the state's population

    Because they have more people

    Because some states have more people

26. We elect a President for how many years?

    Four (4)

27. In what month do we vote for President?*

    November

28. What is the name of the President of the United States now?*

    Barack H. Obama

29. What is the name of the Vice President of the United States now?

    Joseph R. Biden, Jr.

30. If the President can no longer serve, who becomes President?

   The Vice President

31. If both the President and the Vice President can no longer serve, who becomes President?

   The Speaker of the House

32. Who is the Commander in Chief of the military?

   The President

33. Who signs bills to become laws?

   The President

34. Who vetoes bills?

   The President

35. What does the President's Cabinet do?

   Advises the President

36. What are two Cabinet-level positions?

   Secretary of State

   Secretary of Labor

37. What does the judicial branch do?

Reviews laws

Explains laws

Resolves disputes (disagreements)

Decides if a law goes against the Constitution

38. What is the highest court in the United States?

The Supreme Court

39. How many justices are on the Supreme Court?

Nine (9)

40. Who is the Chief Justice of the United States?

John G. Roberts, Jr.

41. Under our Constitution, some powers belong to the federal government. What is one power of the federal government?

Know one of the following:

To print money

To declare war

To create an army

To make treaties

42. Under our Constitution, some powers belong to the states. What is one power of the states?

Provide schooling and education

43. Who is the Governor of your state?

Answers will vary. Residents of the District of Columbia and U.S. territories without a Governor should say "we don't have a Governor."

See Page 60

44. What is the capital of your state?*

See Page 63

45. What are the two major political parties in the United States?*

Democratic and Republican

46. What is the political party of the President now?

Democratic Party

47. What is the name of the Speaker of the House of Representatives now?

Paul Ryan

C: Rights and Responsibilities

48. There are four amendments to the Constitution about who can vote. Describe one of them.

    Citizens eighteen (18) and older can vote.

    Any citizen can vote. (Women and men can vote.)

49. What is one responsibility that is only for United States citizens?*

    Serve on a jury

50. What are two rights only for United States citizens?

    Apply for a federal job

    Vote

51. What are two rights of everyone living in the United States?

    Freedom of expression

    Freedom of speech

52. What do we show loyalty to when we say the Pledge of Allegiance?

    The United States and the flag

53. What is one promise you make when you become a United States citizen?

    Defend the Constitution and laws of the United States

54. How old do citizens have to be to vote?*

Eighteen (18) and older

55. What are two ways that Americans can participate in their democracy?

Vote

Join a political party

56. When is the last day you can send in federal income tax forms?*

April 15

57. When must all men register for the Selective Service?

Between eighteen (18) and twenty-six (26)

AMERICAN HISTORY

A: Colonial Period and Independence

58. What is one reason colonists came to America?

Freedom

Political liberty

59. Who lived in America before the Europeans arrived?

Native Americans

American Indians

60. What group of people was taken to America and sold as slaves?

Africans

61. Why did the colonists fight the British?

Because of high taxes (taxation without representation)

Because the British army stayed in their houses (boarding, quartering)

Because they didn't have self-government

62. Who wrote the Declaration of Independence?

Thomas Jefferson

63. When was the Declaration of Independence adopted?

July 4, 1776

64. There were 13 original states. Name three.

New York

New Jersey

Virginia

65. What happened at the Constitutional Convention?

The Constitution was written.

66. When was the Constitution written?

1787

67. The Federalist Papers supported the passage of the U.S. Constitution. Name one of the writers.

James Madison

68. What is one thing Benjamin Franklin is famous for?

U.S. diplomat

69. Who is the "Father of Our Country"?

George Washington

70. Who was the first President?*

George Washington

71. What territory did the United States buy from France in 1803?

The Louisiana Territory

72. Name one war fought by the United States in the 1800s.

Spanish-American War

73. Name the U.S. war between the North and the South.

The Civil War

74. Name one problem that led to the Civil War.

Slavery

75. What was one important thing that Abraham Lincoln did?*

    Freed the slaves (Emancipation Proclamation)

76. What did the Emancipation Proclamation do?

    Freed the slaves

77. What did Susan B. Anthony do?

    Fought for women's rights

C: Recent American History and Other Important Historical Information

78. Name one war fought by the United States in the 1900s.*

    World War II

79. Who was President during World War I?

    Woodrow Wilson

80. Who was President during the Great Depression and World War II?

    Franklin Roosevelt

81. Who did the United States fight in World War II?

    Japan, Germany and Italy

82. Before he was President, Eisenhower was a general. What war was he in?

    World War II

83. During the Cold War, what was the main concern of the United States?

Communism

84. What movement tried to end racial discrimination?

Civil rights movement

85. What did Martin Luther King, Jr. do?*

Fought for civil rights

86. What major event happened on September 11, 2001 in the United States?

Terrorists attacked the United States.

87. Name one American Indian tribe in the United States.

Cherokee

Navajo

Apache

[Adjudicators will be supplied with a complete list.]

INTEGRATED CIVICS

A: Geography

88. Name one of the two longest rivers in the United States.

Missouri or Mississippi river

89. What ocean is on the West Coast of the United States?

    Pacific Ocean

90. What ocean is on the East Coast of the United States?

    Atlantic Ocean

91. Name one U.S. territory.

    Puerto Rico

92. Name one state that borders Canada.

    New York

93. Name one state that borders Mexico.

    California

94. What is the capital of the United States?*

    Washington, D.C.

95. Where is the Statue of Liberty?*

    New York Harbor

B. Symbols

96. Why does the flag have 13 stripes?

Because there were 13 original colonies

97. Why does the flag have 50 stars?*

Because there is one star for each state

98. What is the name of the national anthem?

The Star-Spangled Banner

C: Holidays

99. When do we celebrate Independence Day?*

   July 4

100. Name two national U.S. holidays.

   Independence Day

   Christmas

SAMPLE WRITTEN SENTENCES

You will be asked to write a sample sentence. Normally you can make up to three (3) errors in writing and still pass the test.
Be careful to listen to each word the examiner reads. Make sure to write each word, even if you think it is not needed grammatically, if the examiner reads a word; please write out every word that is dictated.

1) A senator is elected for 6 years.

2) Joseph Biden is the Vice President of the United States.

3) All people want to be free.

4) America is the land of freedom.

5) All American citizens have the right to vote.

6) America is the home of the brave.

7) America is the land of the free.

8) Barack Obama is the President of the United States.

9) Citizens have the right to vote.

10) Congress is part of the American government.

11) Congress meets in Washington DC.

12) Congress passes laws in the United States.

13) George Washington was the first president.

14) I want to be a citizen of the United States.

15) I want to be an American citizen.

16) I want to become an American so I can vote.

17) It is important for all citizens to vote.

18) Many people come to America for freedom.

19) Many people have died for freedom.

20) Martha Washington was the first lady.

21) Only Congress can declare war.

22) Our Government is divided into three branches.

23) People in America have the right to freedom.

24) People vote for the President in November.

25) The American flag has stars and stripes.

26) The American flag has 13 stripes.

27) The capital of the United States is Washington DC.

28) The colors of the flag are red white and blue.

29) The Constitution is the supreme law of our land.

30) The flag of the United States has 50 stars.

31) The House and Senate are parts of Congress

32) The President enforces the laws.

33) The President has the power of veto.

34) The President is elected every 4 years.

35) The President lives in the White House.

36) The President lives in Washington D.C.

37) The President must be an American citizen.

38) The President must be born in the United States.

39) The President signs bills into law.

40) The stars of the American flag are white.

41) The White House is in Washington, DC.

42) The United States flag is red white and blue.

43) The United States of America has 50 states.

Members of the Senate
Senators of the 114th Congress

Representatives are subject to change.
Find your state to identify your two Senators

Source: http://Senate.gov Updated November 2015

See list below. Answers will vary. For District of Columbia residents and residents of U.S. territories, the answer is that D.C. (or the territory where the applicant lives) has no U.S. Senators.

Alaska: Murkowski, Lisa - (R - AK)   Sullivan, Daniel - (R - AK)

Alabama: Sessions, Jeff - (R - AL)   Shelby, Richard C. - (R - AL)

Arkansas: Boozman, John - (R - AR)   Cotton, Tom - (R - AR)

Arizona: Flake, Jeff - (R - AZ)   McCain, John - (R - AZ)

California: Boxer, Barbara - (D - CA)   Feinstein, Dianne - (D - CA)

Colorado: Bennet, Michael F. - (D - CO)   Gardner, Cory - (R - CO)

Connecticut: Blumenthal, Richard - (D - CT)   Murphy, Christopher - (D - CT)

Delaware: Carper, Thomas R. - (D - DE)   Coons, Christopher A. - (D - DE)

Florida: Nelson, Bill - (D - FL)   Rubio, Marco - (R - FL)

Georgia: Isakson, Johnny - (R - GA)   Perdue, David - (R - GA)

Hawaii: Hirono, Mazie K. - (D - HI)   Schatz, Brian - (D - HI)

Iowa: Ernst, Joni - (R - IA)   Grassley, Chuck - (R - IA)

Idaho: Crapo, Mike - (R - ID)   Risch, James E. - (R - ID)

Illinois: Durbin, Richard J. - (D - IL)   Kirk, Mark - (R - IL)

Indiana: Coats, Daniel - (R - IN)   Donnelly, Joe - (D - IN)

Kansas: Moran, Jerry - (R - KS)   Roberts, Pat - (R - KS)

Kentucky: McConnell, Mitch - (R - KY)   Paul, Rand - (R - KY)

Louisiana: Cassidy, Bill - (R - LA)   Vitter, David - (R - LA)

Massachusetts: Markey, Edward J. - (D - MA)   Warren, Elizabeth - (D - MA)

Maryland: Cardin, Benjamin L. - (D - MD)   Mikulski, Barbara A. - (D - MD)

Maine: Collins, Susan M. - (R - ME)   King, Angus S., Jr. - (I - ME)

Michigan: Peters, Gary - (D - MI)   Stabenow, Debbie - (D - MI)

Minnesota: Franken, Al - (D - MN)   Klobuchar, Amy - (D - MN)

Missouri: Blunt, Roy - (R - MO)   McCaskill, Claire - (D - MO)

Mississippi: Cochran, Thad - (R - MS)   Wicker, Roger F. - (R - MS)

Montana: Tester, Jon - (D - MT)   Daines, Steve - (R - MT)

North Carolina: Burr, Richard - (R - NC)   Tillis, Thom - (R - NC)

North Dakota: Heitkamp, Heidi - (D - ND)   Hoeven, John - (R - ND)

Nebraska: Fischer, Deb - (R - NE)   Sasse, Ben - (R - NE)

New Hampshire: Ayotte, Kelly - (R - NH)   Shaheen, Jeanne - (D - NH)

New Jersey: Booker, Cory A. - (D - NJ)   Menendez, Robert - (D - NJ)

New Mexico: Heinrich, Martin - (D - NM)   Udall, Tom - (D - NM)

Nevada: Heller, Dean - (R - NV)   Reid, Harry - (D - NV)

New York: Gillibrand, Kirsten E. - (D - NY)   Schumer, Charles E. - (D - NY)

Ohio: Brown, Sherrod - (D - OH)   Portman, Rob - (R - OH)

Oklahoma: Inhofe, James M. - (R - OK)   Lankford, James - (R - OK)

Oregon: Merkley, Jeff - (D - OR)   Wyden, Ron - (D - OR)

Pennsylvania: Casey, Robert P., Jr. - (D - PA)   Toomey, Patrick J. - (R - PA)

Rhode Island: Reed, Jack - (D - RI)   Whitehouse, Sheldon - (D - RI)

South Carolina: Graham, Lindsey - (R - SC)   Scott, Tim - (R - SC)

South Carolina: Rounds, Mike - (R - SD)   Thune, John - (R - SD)

Tennessee: Alexander, Lamar - (R - TN)   Corker, Bob - (R - TN)

Texas: Cornyn, John - (R - TX)   Cruz, Ted - (R - TX)

Utah: Hatch, Orrin G. - (R - UT)   Lee, Mike - (R - UT)

Virginia: Kaine, Tim - (D - VA)   Warner, Mark R. - (D - VA)

Vermont: Leahy, Patrick J. - (D - VT)   Sanders, Bernard - (I - VT)

Washington: Cantwell, Maria - (D - WA)   Murray, Patty - (D - WA)

Wisconsin: Baldwin, Tammy - (D - WI)   Johnson, Ron - (R - WI)

West Virginia: Capito, Shelley Moore - (R - WV)   Manchin, Joe, III - (D - WV)

Wyoming: Barrasso, John - (R - WY)   Enzi, Michael B. - (R - WY)

Members of the 114th Congress

Find your state and your District Number to identify your Congressperson. You must determine what district you live in to identify your Representative.
Source: http://www.house.gov/representatives/
Updated November 2015

Alabama

District	Name	Party
1	Byrne, Bradley	R
2	Roby, Martha	R
3	Rogers, Mike	R
4	Aderholt, Robert	R
5	Brooks, Mo	R
6	Palmer, Gary	R
7	Sewell, Terri A.	D

Alaska

District	Name	Party
At Large	Young, Don	R

American Samoa

District	Name	Party

District	Name	Party
At Large	Radewagen, Amata	R

Arizona

District	Name	Party
1	Kirkpatrick, Ann	D
2	McSally, Martha	R
3	Grijalva, Raul	D
4	Gosar, Paul A.	R
5	Salmon, Matt	R
6	Schweikert, David	R
7	Gallego, Ruben	D
8	Franks, Trent	R
9	Sinema, Kyrsten	D

Arkansas

District	Name	Party
1	Crawford, Rick	R
2	Hill, French	R
3	Womack, Steve	R
4	Westerman, Bruce	R

California

District	Name	Party
1	LaMalfa, Doug	R
2	Huffman, Jared	D
3	Garamendi, John	D
4	McClintock, Tom	R
5	Thompson, Mike	D
6	Matsui, Doris O.	D
7	Bera, Ami	D
8	Cook, Paul	R
9	McNerney, Jerry	D
10	Denham, Jeff	R
11	DeSaulnier, Mark	D
12	Pelosi, Nancy	D
13	Lee, Barbara	D
14	Speier, Jackie	D
15	Swalwell, Eric	D
16	Costa, Jim	D
17	Honda, Mike	D
18	Eshoo, Anna G.	D
19	Lofgren, Zoe	D
20	Farr, Sam	D

District	Name	Party
21	Valadao, David	R
22	Nunes, Devin	R
23	McCarthy, Kevin	R
24	Capps, Lois	D
25	Knight, Steve	R
26	Brownley, Julia	D
27	Chu, Judy	D
28	Schiff, Adam	D
29	Cárdenas, Tony	D
30	Sherman, Brad	D
31	Aguilar, Pete	D
32	Napolitano, Grace	D
33	Lieu, Ted	D
34	Becerra, Xavier	D
35	Torres, Norma	D
36	Ruiz, Raul	D
37	Bass, Karen	D
38	Sánchez, Linda	D
39	Royce, Ed	R
40	Roybal-Allard, Lucille	D
41	Takano, Mark	D

District	Name	Party
42	Calvert, Ken	R
43	Waters, Maxine	D
44	Hahn, Janice	D
45	Walters, Mimi	R
46	Sanchez, Loretta	D
47	Lowenthal, Alan	D
48	Rohrabacher, Dana	R
49	Issa, Darrell	R
50	Hunter, Duncan D.	R
51	Vargas, Juan	D
52	Peters, Scott	D
53	Davis, Susan	D

Colorado

District	Name	Party
1	DeGette, Diana	D
2	Polis, Jared	D
3	Tipton, Scott	R
4	Buck, Ken	R
5	Lamborn, Doug	R
6	Coffman, Mike	R

District	Name	Party
7	Perlmutter, Ed	D

Connecticut

District	Name	Party
1	Larson, John B.	D
2	Courtney, Joe	D
3	DeLauro, Rosa L.	D
4	Himes, Jim	D
5	Esty, Elizabeth	D

Delaware

District	Name	Party
At Large	Carney, John	D

District of Columbia

District	Name	Party
At Large	Norton, Eleanor Holmes	D

Florida

District	Name	Party

District	Name	Party
1	Miller, Jeff	R
2	Graham, Gwen	D
3	Yoho, Ted	R
4	Crenshaw, Ander	R
5	Brown, Corrine	D
6	DeSantis, Ron	R
7	Mica, John	R
8	Posey, Bill	R
9	Grayson, Alan	D
10	Webster, Daniel	R
11	Nugent, Richard	R
12	Bilirakis, Gus M.	R
13	Jolly, David	R
14	Castor, Kathy	D
15	Ross, Dennis	R
16	Buchanan, Vern	R
17	Rooney, Tom	R
18	Murphy, Patrick	D
19	Clawson,Curt	R
20	Hastings, Alcee L.	D
21	Deutch, Ted	D

District	Name	Party
22	Frankel, Lois	D
23	Wasserman Schultz, Debbie	D
24	Wilson, Frederica	D
25	Diaz-Balart, Mario	R
26	Curbelo, Carlos	R
27	Ros-Lehtinen, Ileana	R

Georgia

District	Name	Party
1	Carter, Buddy	R
2	Bishop Jr., Sanford D.	D
3	Westmoreland, Lynn A.	R
4	Johnson, Henry C. "Hank" Jr.	D
5	Lewis, John	D
6	Price, Tom	R
7	Woodall, Robert	R
8	Scott, Austin	R
9	Collins, Doug	R
10	Hice, Jody	R
11	Loudermilk, Barry	R
12	Allen, Rick	R

District	Name	Party
13	Scott, David	D
14	Graves, Tom	R

Guam

District	Name	Party
At Large	Bordallo, Madeleine	D

Hawaii

District	Name	Party
1	Takai, Mark	D
2	Gabbard, Tulsi	D

Idaho

District	Name	Party
1	Labrador, Raul R.	R
2	Simpson, Mike	R

Illinois

District	Name	Party
1	Rush, Bobby L.	D
2	Kelly, Robin	D
3	Lipinski, Daniel	D
4	Gutierrez, Luis	D
5	Quigley, Mike	D
6	Roskam, Peter J.	R
7	Davis, Danny K.	D
8	Duckworth, Tammy	D
9	Schakowsky, Jan	D
10	Dold, Bob	R
11	Foster, Bill	D
12	Bost, Mike	R
13	Davis, Rodney	R
14	Hultgren, Randy	R
15	Shimkus, John	R
16	Kinzinger, Adam	R
17	Bustos, Cheri	D
18	LaHood,Darin	R

Indiana

District	Name	Party
1	Visclosky, Peter	D
2	Walorski, Jackie	R
3	Stutzman, Marlin	R
4	Rokita, Todd	R
5	Brooks, Susan W.	R
6	Messer, Luke	R
7	Carson, André	D
8	Bucshon, Larry	R
9	Young, Todd	R

Iowa

District	Name	Party
1	Blum, Rod	R
2	Loebsack, David	D
3	Young, David	R
4	King, Steve	R

Kansas

District	Name	Party
1	Huelskamp, Tim	R
2	Jenkins, Lynn	R
3	Yoder, Kevin	R
4	Pompeo, Mike	R

Kentucky

District	Name	Party
1	Whitfield, Ed	R
2	Guthrie, S. Brett	R
3	Yarmuth, John A.	D
4	Massie, Thomas	R
5	Rogers, Harold	R
6	Barr, Andy	R

Louisiana

District	Name	Party
1	Scalise, Steve	R
2	Richmond, Cedric	D
3	Boustany Jr., Charles W.	R

District	Name	Party
4	Fleming, John	R
5	Abraham, Ralph	R
6	Graves, Garret	R

Maine

District	Name	Party
1	Pingree, Chellie	D
2	Poliquin, Bruce	R

Maryland

District	Name	Party
1	Harris, Andy	R
2	Ruppersberger, C. A. Dutch	D
3	Sarbanes, John P.	D
4	Edwards, Donna F.	D
5	Hoyer, Steny H.	D
6	Delaney, John	D
7	Cummings, Elijah	D
8	Van Hollen, Chris	D

Massachusetts

District	Name	Party
1	Neal, Richard E.	D
2	McGovern, James	D
3	Tsongas, Niki	D
4	Kennedy III, Joseph P.	D
5	Clark, Katherine	D
6	Moulton, Seth	D
7	Capuano, Michael E.	D
8	Lynch, Stephen F.	D
9	Keating, William	D

Michigan

District	Name	Party
1	Benishek, Dan	R
2	Huizenga, Bill	R
3	Amash, Justin	R
4	Moolenaar, John	R
5	Kildee, Daniel	D
6	Upton, Fred	R
7	Walberg, Tim	R

District	Name	Party
8	Bishop, Mike	R
9	Levin, Sander	D
10	Miller, Candice	R
11	Trott, Dave	R
12	Dingell, Debbie	D
13	Conyers Jr., John	D
14	Lawrence, Brenda	D

Minnesota

District	Name	Party
1	Walz, Timothy J.	D
2	Kline, John	R
3	Paulsen, Erik	R
4	McCollum, Betty	D
5	Ellison, Keith	D
6	Emmer, Tom	R
7	Peterson, Collin C.	D
8	Nolan, Rick	D

Mississippi

District	Name	Party
1	Kelly, Trent	R
2	Thompson, Bennie G.	D
3	Harper, Gregg	R
4	Palazzo, Steven	R

Missouri

District	Name	Party
1	Clay Jr., William "Lacy"	D
2	Wagner, Ann	R
3	Luetkemeyer, Blaine	R
4	Hartzler, Vicky	R
5	Cleaver, Emanuel	D
6	Graves, Sam	R
7	Long, Billy	R
8	Smith, Jason	R

Montana

District	Name	Party
At Large	Zinke, Ryan	R

Nebraska

District	Name	Party
1	Fortenberry, Jeff	R
2	Ashford, Brad	D
3	Smith, Adrian	R

Nevada

District	Name	Party
1	Titus, Dina	D
2	Amodei, Mark	R
3	Heck, Joe	R
4	Hardy, Cresent	R

New Hampshire

District	Name	Party
1	Guinta, Frank	R
2	Kuster, Ann	D

New Jersey

District	Name	Party
1	Norcross, Donald	D
2	LoBiondo, Frank	R
3	MacArthur, Tom	R
4	Smith, Chris	R
5	Garrett, Scott	R
6	Pallone Jr., Frank	D
7	Lance, Leonard	R
8	Sires, Albio	D
9	Pascrell Jr., Bill	D
10	Payne Jr., Donald	D
11	Frelinghuysen, Rodney	R
12	Watson Coleman, Bonnie	D

New Mexico

District	Name	Party
1	Lujan Grisham, Michelle	D
2	Pearce, Steve	R
3	Lujan, Ben R.	D

New York

District	Name	Party
1	Zeldin, Lee	R
2	King, Pete	R
3	Israel, Steve	D
4	Rice, Kathleen	D
5	Meeks, Gregory W.	D
6	Meng, Grace	D
7	Velázquez, Nydia M.	D
8	Jeffries, Hakeem	D
9	Clarke, Yvette D.	D
10	Nadler, Jerrold	D
11	Donovan, Daniel	R
12	Maloney, Carolyn	D
13	Rangel, Charles B.	D
14	Crowley, Joseph	D
15	Serrano, José E.	D
16	Engel, Eliot	D
17	Lowey, Nita	D
18	Maloney, Sean Patrick	D
19	Gibson, Chris	R
20	Tonko, Paul D.	D

District	Name	Party
21	Stefanik, Elise	R
22	Hanna, Richard	R
23	Reed, Tom	R
24	Katko, John	R
25	Slaughter, Louise	D
26	Higgins, Brian	D
27	Collins, Chris	R

North Carolina

District	Name	Party
1	Butterfield, G.K.	D
2	Ellmers, Renee	R
3	Jones, Walter B.	R
4	Price, David	D
5	Foxx, Virginia	R
6	Walker, Mark	R
7	Rouzer, David	R
8	Hudson, Richard	R
9	Pittenger, Robert	R
10	McHenry, Patrick T.	R
11	Meadows, Mark	R

District	Name	Party
12	Adams, Alma	D
13	Holding, George	R

North Dakota

District	Name	Party
At Large	Cramer, Kevin	R

Northern Mariana Islands

District	Name	Party
At Large	Sablan, Gregorio	D

Ohio

District	Name	Party
1	Chabot, Steve	R
2	Wenstrup, Brad	R
3	Beatty, Joyce	D
4	Jordan, Jim	R
5	Latta, Robert E.	R
6	Johnson, Bill	R
7	Gibbs, Bob	R

District	Name	Party
8	Boehner, John A.	R
9	Kaptur, Marcy	D
10	Turner, Michael	R
11	Fudge, Marcia L.	D
12	Tiberi, Pat	R
13	Ryan, Tim	D
14	Joyce, David	R
15	Stivers, Steve	R
16	Renacci, Jim	R

Oklahoma

District	Name	Party
1	Bridenstine, Jim	R
2	Mullin, Markwayne	R
3	Lucas, Frank	R
4	Cole, Tom	R
5	Russell, Steve	R

Oregon

District	Name	Party
1	Bonamici, Suzanne	D
2	Walden, Greg	R
3	Blumenauer, Earl	D
4	DeFazio, Peter	D
5	Schrader, Kurt	D

Pennsylvania

District	Name	Party
1	Brady, Robert	D
2	Fattah, Chaka	D
3	Kelly, Mike	R
4	Perry, Scott	R
5	Thompson, Glenn W.	R
6	Costello, Ryan	R
7	Meehan, Pat	R
8	Fitzpatrick, Michael G.	R
9	Shuster, Bill	R
10	Marino, Tom	R
11	Barletta, Lou	R

District	Name	Party
12	Rothfus, Keith	R
13	Boyle, Brendan	D
14	Doyle, Mike	D
15	Dent, Charles W.	R
16	Pitts, Joseph R.	R
17	Cartwright, Matthew	D
18	Murphy, Tim	R

Puerto Rico

District	Name	Party
At Large	Pierluisi, Pedro	D

Rhode Island

District	Name	Party
1	Cicilline, David	D
2	Langevin, Jim	D

South Carolina

District	Name	Party
1	Sanford, Mark	R
2	Wilson, Joe	R
3	Duncan, Jeff	R
4	Gowdy, Trey	R
5	Mulvaney, Mick	R
6	Clyburn, James E.	D
7	Rice, Tom	R

South Dakota

District	Name	Party
At Large	Noem, Kristi	R

Tennessee

District	Name	Party
1	Roe, Phil	R
2	Duncan Jr., John J.	R
3	Fleischmann, Chuck	R
4	DesJarlais, Scott	R
5	Cooper, Jim	D

District	Name	Party
6	Black, Diane	R
7	Blackburn, Marsha	R
8	Fincher, Stephen	R
9	Cohen, Steve	D

Texas

District	Name	Party
1	Gohmert, Louie	R
2	Poe, Ted	R
3	Johnson, Sam	R
4	Ratcliffe, John	R
5	Hensarling, Jeb	R
6	Barton, Joe	R
7	Culberson, John	R
8	Brady, Kevin	R
9	Green, Al	D
10	McCaul, Michael T.	R
11	Conaway, K. Michael	R
12	Granger, Kay	R
13	Thornberry, Mac	R
14	Weber, Randy	R

District	Name	Party
15	Hinojosa, Rubén	D
16	O'Rourke, Beto	D
17	Flores, Bill	R
18	Jackson Lee, Sheila	D
19	Neugebauer, Randy	R
20	Castro, Joaquin	D
21	Smith, Lamar	R
22	Olson, Pete	R
23	Hurd, Will	R
24	Marchant, Kenny	R
25	Williams, Roger	R
26	Burgess, Michael	R
27	Farenthold, Blake	R
28	Cuellar, Henry	D
29	Green, Gene	D
30	Johnson, Eddie Bernice	D
31	Carter, John	R
32	Sessions, Pete	R
33	Veasey, Marc	D
34	Vela, Filemon	D
35	Doggett, Lloyd	D

District	Name	Party
36	Babin, Brian	R

Utah

District	Name	Party
1	Bishop, Rob	R
2	Stewart, Chris	R
3	Chaffetz, Jason	R
4	Love, Mia	R

Vermont

District	Name	Party
At Large	Welch, Peter	D

Virgin Islands

District	Name	Party
At Large	Plaskett, Stacey	D

Virginia

District	Name	Party
1	Wittman, Robert J.	R
2	Rigell, Scott	R
3	Scott, Robert C.	D
4	Forbes, J. Randy	R
5	Hurt, Robert	R
6	Goodlatte, Bob	R
7	Brat, Dave	R
8	Beyer, Don	D
9	Griffith, Morgan	R
10	Comstock, Barbara	R
11	Connolly, Gerald E. "Gerry"	D

Washington

District	Name	Party
1	DelBene, Suzan	D
2	Larsen, Rick	D
3	Herrera Beutler, Jaime	R
4	Newhouse, Dan	R
5	McMorris Rodgers, Cathy	R

District	Name	Party
6	Kilmer, Derek	D
7	McDermott, Jim	D
8	Reichert, David G.	R
9	Smith, Adam	D
10	Heck, Denny	D

West Virginia

District	Name	Party
1	McKinley, David	R
2	Mooney, Alex	R
3	Jenkins, Evan	R

Wisconsin

District	Name	Party
1	Ryan, Paul D.	R
2	Pocan, Mark	D
3	Kind, Ron	D
4	Moore, Gwen	D
5	Sensenbrenner, F. James	R
6	Grothman, Glenn	R

District	Name	Party
7	Duffy, Sean P.	R
8	Ribble, Reid	R

Wyoming

District	Name	Party
At Large	Lummis, Cynthia M.	R

List of State Governors

Governors are subject to change

Source: http://en.wikipedia.org/wiki/List_of_current_United_States_governors
November 2015

Alabama Governor Robert Bentley

Alaska Governor Bill Walker

American Samoa Governor Lolo Matalasi Moliga

Arizona Governor Doug Ducey

Arkansas Governor Asa Hutchinson

California Governor Edmund G. Brown

Colorado Governor John Hickenlooper

Connecticut Governor Dan Malloy

Delaware Governor Jack Markell

Florida Governor Rick Scott

Georgia Governor Nathan Deal

Guam Governor Eddie Baza Calvo

Hawaii Governor David Ige

Idaho Governor C. L. "Butch" Otter

Illinois Governor Bruce Rauner

Indiana Governor Mike Pence

Iowa Governor Terry E. Branstad

Kansas Governor Sam Brownback

Kentucky Governor Steven L. Beshear

Louisiana Governor Bobby Jindal

Maine Governor Paul LePage

Maryland Governor Martin O'Malley

Massachusetts Governor Charlie Baker

Michigan Governor Rick Snyder

Minnesota Governor Mark Dayton

Mississippi Governor Phil Bryant

Missouri Governor Jeremiah W. (Jay) Nixon

Montana Governor Steve Bullock

Nebraska Governor Pete Ricketts

Nevada Governor Brian Sandoval

New Hampshire Governor Maggie Hassan

New Jersey Governor Christopher Christie

New Mexico Governor Susana Martinez

New York Governor Andrew Cuomo

North Carolina Governor Pat McCrory

North Dakota Governor Jack Dalrymple

Northern Mariana Islands Governor Eloy Inos

Ohio Governor John Kasich

Oklahoma Governor Mary Fallin

Oregon Governor John A. Kitzhaber, M.D.

Pennsylvania Governor Tom Corbett

Puerto Rico Governor Alejandro Javier García Padilla

Rhode Island Governor Gina Raimondo

South Carolina Governor Nikki R. Haley

South Dakota Governor Dennis Daugaard

Tennessee Governor Bill Haslam

Texas Governor Rick Perry

Utah Governor Gary Richard Herbert

Vermont Governor Peter Shumlin

Virginia Governor Terry McAuliffe

Virgin Islands Governor Kenneth Mapp

Washington Governor Jay Inslee

West Virginia Governor Earl Ray Tomblin

Wisconsin Governor Scott Walker

Wyoming Governor Matthew Mead

List of State Capitols

Alabama - Montgomery

Alaska - Juneau

Arizona - Phoenix

Arkansas - Little Rock

California - Sacramento

Colorado - Denver

Connecticut - Hartford

Delaware - Dover

Florida - Tallahassee

Georgia - Atlanta

Hawaii - Honolulu

Idaho - Boise

Illinois - Springfield

Indiana - Indianapolis

Iowa - Des Moines

Kansas - Topeka

Kentucky - Frankfort

Louisiana - Baton Rouge

Maine - Augusta

Maryland - Annapolis

Massachusetts - Boston

Michigan - Lansing

Minnesota - St. Paul

Mississippi - Jackson

Missouri - Jefferson City

Montana - Helena

Nebraska - Lincoln

Nevada - Carson City

New Hampshire - Concord

New Jersey - Trenton

New Mexico - Santa Fe

New York - Albany

North Carolina - Raleigh

North Dakota - Bismarck

Ohio - Columbus

Oklahoma - Oklahoma City

Oregon - Salem

Pennsylvania - Harrisburg

Rhode Island - Providence

South Carolina - Columbia

South Dakota - Pierre

Tennessee - Nashville

Texas - Austin

Utah - Salt Lake City

Vermont - Montpelier

Virginia - Richmond

Washington - Olympia

West Virginia - Charleston

Wisconsin - Madison

Wyoming - Cheyenne

ABOUT THE AUTHOR

Mike Swedenberg saw a need to assemble a study guide to help those persons wishing to immigrate to the United States whose second language is English. This study guide is annotated with the names of current Representatives that all applicants must know. The list is current for State Governors, US Senators and US Congressmen. This list will be updated at each election cycle.

Other books by the Author
A New York Wedding – a novel
Bully Boss – a novel
The Road Warrior a sales manual
Advertising Copywriting and the Unique Selling Proposition

Made in the USA
Charleston, SC
24 November 2015